W9-CFY-904

SWEET SCOOPS
LOW-FAT
FROZEN DESSERTS

COLE GROUP

© 1996 Cole Group, Inc.

Front cover photograph: Victor Budnik
Page 7: Krups North America, Inc.
Pages 9 and 49: Browne & Co. Ltd., 100 Esna Park Dr.,
Markham, Ontario L3R 1E3 Canada (905) 475-6104
Nutritional Analysis: MasterCook II, Arion Software Inc.

Cole Publishing Group, Inc.
1330 N. Dutton Ave., Suite 103
Santa Rosa, CA 95401
(800) 959-2717 (707) 526-2682
FAX (707) 526-2687

Printed in Hong Kong

G   F   E   D   C   B   A
2   1   0   9   8   7   6

ISBN 1-56426-818-7

Library of Congress Catalog Card Number 95-45658

Distributed to the book trade by Publishers Group West

Cole books are available for quantity purchases for sales promotions, premiums, fund-raising, or educational use. For more information on *Sweet Scoops: Low-Fat Frozen Desserts* or other Cole's Cooking Companion books, please write or call the publisher.

CONTENTS

THE REAL SCOOP

*P*astel ovals of sorbet . . . Miniature glaciers of granita . . . Icy frappes and frosty ice cream sodas . . . Luscious mounds of frozen yogurt . . . Glistening bombes . . . Fire-and-ice flambés . . . Exquisite frozen mousses and soufflés . . . These and dozens of other low-fat delights are as close as your own kitchen.

SWEET FREEZE: A PRIMER

From Popsicles© to Peach Melba, frozen specialties run the gamut from simple to sophisticated. Gelato, glace, ice cream, nieve, granita, helado, ice milk, sherbet, sorbet, sorbetto, frozen yogurt, water ice—names and distinctions for these icy delights blur across cultural boundaries, reflecting their enormous popularity worldwide. Here are some broad definitions to help sort it all out:

Ice Cream   Made from either a cooked custard or uncooked base. Ice cream made with eggs and cream is higher in fat than ice "cream" made with skim milk (low-fat or nonfat). As a rule, the higher the fat content of the base mixture, the creamier the texture; incorporating gelatin, egg substitutes, or lecithin (an emulsifier made from soybeans) into mixtures made with skim milk makes the texture creamier.

Gelato   A dense, firm Italian ice cream containing less air than French glace or American ice cream. Achieving a gelato-like consistency at home is easy with a hand-cranked canister freezer (see photo on page 9), which whips very little air into the base during freezing.

Granita   A type of water ice (sherbet) with a slightly grainy texture, the result of freezing without constant churning. Granita is traditionally served slightly thawed and slushy, but if you like a smoother texture similar to a churn-frozen sherbet, purée it in a food processor shortly before serving.

Ice   A generic term for a sherbet; milk ice is sherbet to which a small amount of milk or cream has been added.

Sherbet, Sorbet, Sorbetto   A water ice usually made with fruit (or fruit juice) and sugar syrup. Other names for this product include ice, water ice, Italian ice, and fruit ice. To further complicate the issue, in some parts of the United States "sherbet" is the name for milk ice; "sorbet" is water ice. A small serving of wine- or citrus-flavored sorbet—a palate cleanser—is sometimes served between courses, to freshen the taste buds.

Frozen Yogurt   Has a smooth texture similar to ice cream and a slightly acidic taste that complements fruit particularly well.

The recipes in "Skinny Dipping" (see pages 12–39) contain less than 1 gram of fat per serving; however, all the recipes in this book conform to current nutritional guidelines recommending that no more than 30% of the total daily caloric intake should come from fat. Nutritional data (number of calories and amount of fat, percentage of fat from calories, and cholesterol contained in the serving size indicated) follow each recipe. The nutritional values do not include optional ingredients or inexact quantities of foods used for garnishing.

DREAM MACHINES

For anyone who loves frozen desserts, the new generation of ice cream freezers is pure dreamery, making it easier than ever before to enjoy your favorite frozen specialties at home anytime you like, not just on special occasions. Compact, convenient, and highly efficient, these machines stand ready to crank out icy pleasures at a moment's notice.

Although a few recipes in this book are made by still-freezing the base mixture in the freezer compartment of a refrigerator, most employ churn-freezing, using one of the following types of hand- or electric-powered ice cream makers:

Salt-and-Ice Bucket Freezer Licking the dasher after hand-cranking the ice cream churn is a sweet childhood memory for many ice cream enthusiasts. This type of machine features a bucket fitted with a lidded metal canister that holds the base mixture. Powered by a hand crank or electric motor, the canister rotates continuously, surrounded by ice and rock salt, causing the contents of the canister to freeze as it is churned by a stationary dasher. This machine requires about 20–30 minutes of cranking for each batch. The slower the freezing process, the finer the texture; fast freezing yields an icy, coarse texture. One variation on this type of machine needs no salt or ice because it operates inside the freezer compartment of a refrigerator, with the power cord snaking out through the closed door.

Prechilled Canister Freezer This type of machine features a coolant sealed in a hollow metal canister. After the canister has chilled in the freezer compartment of a refrigerator for at least 8 hours, the base mixture is poured into the center of the canister, and the dasher assembly and lid are fitted into place. Hand-powered models (such as the one on page 9) have a crank that is rotated every 2 or 3 minutes until the mixture freezes

(usually in about 15 minutes). Electric models require about the same amount of time.

Self-Contained Refrigerated Freezer The Maserati of ice cream makers, this Italian design boasts a countertop unit with built-in refrigeration and a motorized dasher. It is the easiest to use (and the most expensive), producing the smoothest texture of any machine for home use.

THE SKINNY ON LOW-FAT FROZEN DESSERTS

- You can make most base mixtures up to several days ahead, store them in the refrigerator, and freeze them shortly before serving. Chilling the base mixture before freezing it helps increase the volume of the finished product.

- Sorbets made with wine or spirits tend to be grainy because alcohol inhibits freezing. For a smooth sorbet, add the alcohol toward the end of the freezing process, if possible.

- Nondairy (soy or rice) beverage products can replace milk in most recipes.

- Store frozen desserts in covered, airtight containers to prevent absorption of odors from other foods. Pressing plastic film directly onto the surface of the product before replacing the lid helps prevent the formation of ice crystals.

RECIPES AND TECHNIQUES

*L*ose yourself in the vivid colors, smooth
textures, and intense flavors of a frozen
fantasy. Plunge into a scoop of sorbet,
indulge in a slice of frozen pie, or sip a
bottomless ice cream soda. The more than
50 recipes in this book are a frozen dessert
lover's dream come true and—better yet—
they are all low in fat. So go ahead, there's
no sin in savoring these icy-cool sensations.

SKINNY DIPPING

Let your taste buds delight in the flavor of cool raspberry sorbet, slushy granita spiked with espresso, or an icy frappe fragrant with ripe peaches. You can frolic guiltlessly through this chilly wonderland because the recipes in this section are not only sinfully delicious, they contain less than 1 gram of fat per serving.

PAPAYA SORBET

Streamline the preparation of this sorbet by first freezing the papaya, then puréeing it in a blender or food processor.

4 cups	sliced papayas	900 ml
¼ cup	freshly squeezed orange juice	60 ml
¼ cup	freshly squeezed lime juice	60 ml
to taste	sugar	to taste
pinch	salt	pinch
as needed	lime wedges (optional), for garnish	as needed

1. Spread papaya in one layer on a baking sheet. Freeze, uncovered, until frozen solid.

2. Place papaya and orange and lime juices in a blender or food processor. Process until smooth, stopping to scrape work bowl as necessary. If your machine struggles to process the frozen papaya, let fruit stand 10–15 minutes at room temperature to thaw slightly. Depending on the size of your blender or food processor, you may have to process fruit in several batches.

3. Add sugar to taste and salt. Mix thoroughly by hand or in food processor. Serve at once, garnished with lime wedges, if desired.

Makes about 4 cups (900 ml), 4 servings.
Each serving: cal 262, fat .3 g, cal from fat 9%, chol 0 mg

RASPBERRY SORBET

This intensely flavored sorbet stores well for up to two weeks. Strain the raspberries through a fine sieve to remove the seeds. Avoid grinding the seeds against the sieve, as this will cloud both the color and the flavor of the sorbet.

2 pints	fresh raspberries	450 g
1 cup	Simple Sugar Syrup (see page 16)	250 ml
1½ tbl	lemon juice	1½ tbl

Put raspberries through a sieve or food mill to remove seeds. In a blender or food processor, blend with Simple Sugar Syrup and lemon juice until evenly mixed. Transfer to an ice cream machine and freeze according to manufacturer's instructions.

Makes about 4 cups (900 ml), 4 servings.
Each serving: cal 191, fat .7 g, cal from fat 3%, chol 0 mg

STRAWBERRY SORBET

This luscious dessert deserves very ripe, sweet berries (see photo on page 65).

2½ pints	strawberries, hulled	1.1 l
1 cup	Simple Sugar Syrup (see page 16)	250 ml
1 tbl	lemon juice	1 tbl

Purée strawberries in food processor; strain through sieve or food mill to remove seeds. Stir about three fourths of the cold sugar syrup into the purée; add lemon juice. Taste and add more syrup if necessary. Transfer to an ice cream machine and freeze according to manufacturer's instructions.

Makes about 4 cups (900 ml), 4 servings.
Each serving: cal 467, fat .5 g, cal from fat 1%, chol 0 mg

SIMPLE SUGAR SYRUP

The characteristic flavor and fine texture of most sorbets is the result of a basic syrup made by boiling sugar and water to a specific density. The density of the sugar syrup affects the texture and flavor of sherbet or sorbet. Too much sugar makes the finished product overly soft; too little makes it unpleasantly hard.

French sorbets, made with a fairly light syrup, have an intense fruit flavor and slightly grainy texture; Italian sorbettos, made with a heavier sugar syrup, are both sweeter and smoother. This traditional simple sugar syrup produces sorbet that falls somewhere between the French and Italian styles.

2 cups	sugar	500 ml

1. In a medium-sized saucepan over high heat, cook sugar and 1 cup (250 ml) water, stirring constantly, until sugar dissolves and mixture reaches a full, rolling boil.

2. Immediately remove from heat and cool to room temperature. Strain through a fine sieve into a jar or bowl. Cover and refrigerate until needed. Sugar syrup should always be well cooled (to about 40°F or 4°C) before being used. Store in refrigerator for up to 2–3 weeks.

Makes about 2 cups (500 ml) syrup.

SOFT-BALL SUGAR SYRUP

Some of the recipes in this book (see Frozen Pumpkin Mousse on page 44) call for heating simple sugar syrup until it reaches 234°F–240°F (112°C–116°C). At this temperature a small spoonful of the hot syrup will form a soft ball when it is dropped into ice water, then rubbed between finger and thumb. If the syrup continues to cook beyond this point, it caramelizes and becomes brittle.

GRAPE SORBET

Experiment with juice from different types of both table and wine grapes for a variety of flavors.

1 cup	Simple Sugar Syrup (see page 16), chilled	250 ml
1 cup	grape juice (preferably from wine grapes)	250 ml
2 tbl	raspberry-flavored vinegar	2 tbl
as needed	mint leaves, for garnish	as needed

Combine syrup, juice, and vinegar. Transfer to an ice cream machine and freeze according to manufacturer's instructions. Garnish with mint leaves before serving.

Makes about 2 cups (500 ml), 4 servings.
Each serving: cal 169, fat .1 g, cal from fat 0%, chol 0 mg

FRESH APPLE SORBET

The flavor of this sorbet will vary with the variety of apple you choose.

6 small	tart green apples, cored and peeled	6 small
1 cup	Simple Sugar Syrup (see page 16)	250 ml
1 tbl	lemon juice	1 tbl

1. Blend apples in a blender or food processor with syrup and lemon juice until completely smooth.

2. Transfer to an ice cream machine and freeze according to manufacturer's instructions.

Makes about 4 cups (900 ml), 4 servings.
Each serving: cal 223, fat .2 g, cal from fat 1%, chol 0 mg

NECTARINE SORBET

For a cool, refreshing ending to any meal, serve this tangy dessert garnished with fresh mint leaves.

4 cups	nectarines, sliced and peeled	900 ml
½ cup	freshly squeezed orange juice	125 ml
to taste	sugar	to taste
pinch	salt	pinch
as needed	mint leaves, for garnish	as needed

1. Spread sliced nectarines in one layer on a baking sheet. Freeze, uncovered, until frozen solid.

2. Place frozen nectarines and orange juice in a blender or food processor. Process until smooth, stopping to scrape work bowl as necessary. If your machine struggles to process the frozen nectarines, let fruit stand 10–15 minutes at room temperature to thaw slightly. Depending on the size of your blender or food processor, you may have to process nectarines in several batches.

3. Add sugar to taste and salt. Mix thoroughly by hand or in food processor. Serve at once, garnished with mint leaves, or return to freezer for up to 1 hour.

Makes about 3 cups (700 ml), 4 servings.
Each serving: cal 81, fat .7 g, cal from fat 7%, chol 0 mg

BLOOD ORANGE SORBET

Blood oranges, as well as common oranges and navel oranges, belong to the sweet (as opposed to bitter) orange variety. Blood oranges develop pink or red flesh, juice, and rind. The distinctive flavor, usually described as resembling that of berries, makes the blood orange one of the most delicious of all oranges.

| 1 cup | sugar | 250 ml |
| 2 cups | freshly squeezed blood orange juice | 500 ml |

1. In a saucepan bring sugar and 1 cup (250 ml) water to a boil, then simmer 5 minutes. Set aside to cool about 10 minutes.

2. Combine sugar syrup with blood orange juice and chill well. Transfer to an ice cream machine and freeze according to manufacturer's instructions.

Makes about 3 cups (700 ml), 4 servings.
Each serving: cal 249, fat .3 g, cal from fat 1%, chol 0 mg

FRESH FRUIT SHELLS

For special occasions you can dress up fruit sorbets by serving them in the shells created from the same fruits from which the sorbets were made. Good choices for fruit shells include:

- *apples*
- *apricots*
- *giant strawberries*
- *grapefruits*
- *guavas*
- *kiwifruits*

- *lemons*
- *limes*
- *mangoes*
- *oranges*
- *peaches*
- *plums*

Simply scoop out the center of the fruits, freeze the shells, and then fill them with the appropriate sorbets. Wrap tightly in plastic film and return to the freezer until serving time.

CRANBERRY SORBET

This sorbet is ideal for a formal holiday dinner party. Serve it in small portions, in hollowed-out frozen lemon or orange shells (see page 21) garnished with mint leaves.

1 cup	cranberries	250 ml
1 cup	unsweetened cranberry juice	250 ml
1 cup	sugar	250 ml

1. In a saucepan cook cranberries, cranberry juice, and 1 cup (250 ml) water over medium heat until berries pop open and mixture thickens. Remove from heat, cool, and strain through a sieve or food mill.

2. Add enough water to mixture to make 3 cups (700 ml). Return to saucepan, add sugar, and cook over low heat until sugar is dissolved. Cool.

3. Transfer to an ice cream machine and freeze according to manufacturer's instructions.

Makes about 3 cups (700 ml), 4 servings.
Each serving: cal 241, fat .1 g, cal from fat 0%, chol 0 mg

SWEDISH SORBET

This dessert is popular in Sweden, a country known for its berries and its aquavit, a Scandinavian liquor flavored with caraway seeds.

1 pkg (12 oz)	cranberries	1 pkg (350 g)
¾ cup	sugar	175 ml
½ cup	freshly squeezed orange juice	125 ml
3 tbl	lemon juice	3 tbl
2 tsp	lemon zest, finely chopped	2 tsp
½ cup	milk, skim	125 ml
½ cup	aquavit	125 ml

1. In a saucepan bring cranberries, 1 cup (250 ml) water, sugar, orange juice, lemon juice, and lemon zest to a boil. Cook about 10 minutes, stirring occasionally, until berries have popped and mixture is thick. Remove from heat and let cool.

2. In a blender or food processor, purée mixture until it is liquid. Add milk and aquavit; mix well.

3. Transfer to an ice cream machine and freeze according to manufacturer's instructions.

Makes about 4 cups (900 ml), 4 servings.
Each serving: cal 279, fat .3 g, cal from fat 1%, chol 1 mg

WINE SORBET

This delicate palate refresher or frozen dessert can be made from just about any table wine except a really tannic red. You can also use a sweet wine, but reduce the sugar in the syrup by a tablespoon. Riesling or White Zinfandel would be good wines to start with, but feel free to experiment with various whites, rosés, and reds.

Alcohol affects the freezing process, so don't omit the step of boiling half the wine with the syrup one day before you plan to serve the sorbet. This procedure removes some, but not all, of the alcohol, giving the sorbet just the right texture and flavor. The sorbet does not keep well, as it tends to separate in the freezer.

| ½ cup | sugar | 125 ml |
| 1 cup | dry or slightly sweet table wine | 250 ml |

1. A day ahead, in a saucepan combine 1 cup (250 ml) water, sugar, and half the wine. Stir to dissolve sugar; bring to a boil. Reduce heat and simmer 3 minutes. Allow syrup to cool.

2. Add remaining wine to syrup. Pour into a shallow container and freeze overnight.

3. Two to four hours before serving, remove frozen mixture from freezer. Transfer to a food processor and process until smooth, about 20–30 seconds. Return mixture to freezer container or individual serving glasses and freeze to set.

4. Remove sorbet from the freezer 5–10 minutes before serving to soften slightly.

Serves 6.
Each serving: cal 91, fat 0 g, cal from fat 0%, chol 0 mg

MARGARITA SORBET

This cocktail-in-a-dessert makes a festive ending to a Mexican meal.

1⅛ cups	sugar	280 ml
⅓ cup	lime juice (juice of 4–5 limes)	85 ml
1 tbl	lime pulp (scooped from juiced limes with a teaspoon), seeds removed	1 tbl
2 tbl	gold or añejo tequila	2 tbl
2 tsp	triple sec (citrus liqueur)	2 tsp
2	egg whites	2

1. In a saucepan over medium heat, combine sugar and 2 cups (500 ml) water. Heat until sugar melts and mixture starts to bubble. Cook 10 minutes longer, regulating heat until mixture bubbles gently. Remove from heat and cool slightly.

2. Stir lime juice, lime pulp, tequila, and triple sec into sugar mixture. Pour into a freezerproof serving dish. Still-freeze in freezer until the mixture starts to set (about 1 hour). Remove from freezer and stir briskly with a fork. Return to freezer and chill until mixture is thick and grainy (about 2 more hours), stirring again every half hour or so to keep mixture from freezing solid.

3. Beat egg whites until soft peaks form (see page 43). Remove mixture from freezer and beat very rapidly to a fluff (using a fork or electric mixer). Immediately fold in egg whites. Return mixture to freezer and chill at least 1 more hour before serving.

Serves 8.
Each serving: cal 129, fat 0 g, cal from fat 0%, chol 0 mg

BLACK-VELVET ICE

This adult dessert or palate refresher offers a tart combination of flavors.

¾ cup	Guinness Stout, chilled	175 ml
¾ cup	extra-dry Champagne, chilled	175 ml
1½ cups	Simple Sugar Syrup, chilled (see page 16)	350 ml
1 tbl	lemon juice	1 tbl

Combine all ingredients. Transfer to an ice cream machine and freeze according to manufacturer's instructions.

Makes about 3 cups (700 ml), 6 servings.
Each serving: cal 167, fat 0 g, cal from fat 0%, chol 0 mg

SPIRITED SORBETS

Give your favorite sorbet extra sparkle by adding a tablespoon or two (or to taste) of spirits to the recipe. The following combinations work very well:

- *apple sorbet with calvados*

- *apricot sorbet with amaretto or apricot brandy*

- *kiwifruit sorbet with Riesling wine*

- *lemon sorbet with vodka or gin*

- *lime sorbet with tequila*

- *orange sorbet with Cointreau*

- *peach sorbet with rum*

- *pear sorbet with pear liqueur*

- *plum sorbet with kirsch*

- *strawberry sorbet with white crème de menthe*

KUMQUAT ICE

Golden, sweet-sour kumquats resemble miniature oranges. Rarely more than an inch long, this citrus fruit has a short season; be sure to take advantage of their unique flavor while they're available. The skin is the sweetest part of kumquats, so never peel them.

2 cups	fresh kumquats	500 ml
1¼ cups	sugar	300 ml
1½ cups	freshly squeezed orange juice	350 ml
3 tbl	lemon juice	3 tbl

1. Halve kumquats and purée in a blender or food processor. Transfer to a saucepan, add sugar and bring to a boil over medium heat. Reduce heat and simmer 15 minutes, stirring frequently.

2. Remove from heat and add 2 cups (500 ml) water, orange juice, and lemon juice. Strain into a clean bowl and cool thoroughly.

3. Transfer to an ice cream machine and freeze according to manufacturer's instructions.

Makes about 4 cups (900 ml), 4 servings.
Each serving: cal 356, fat .3 g, cal from fat 1%, chol 0 mg

Fig and Rum Ice in Papaya Shells

This dessert offers a glorious combination of flavors and colors. Figs are extraordinarily sweet when fully ripe, with flesh that ranges from gold to deep red.

12	plump fresh figs	12
2 tbl	rum	2 tbl
1 tbl	lemon juice	1 tbl
2 cups	Simple Sugar Syrup (see page 16)	500 ml
3	ripe papayas, halved and seeded	3
as needed	fresh mint leaves, for garnish	as needed

1. Gently wash and trim figs. Purée in a blender or food processor. Chill purée well.

2. Mix together chilled fig purée, rum, lemon juice, and sugar syrup. Transfer to an ice cream machine and freeze according to manufacturer's instructions. Spoon ice mixture into papaya halves and garnish with fresh mint leaves.

Serves 6.
Each serving: cal 274, fat .5 g, cal from fat 2%, chol 0 mg

Minted Pink Grapefruit Ice

This easy-to-prepare, delicately flavored dessert is the perfect finale for a sumptuous brunch.

⅔ cup	sugar	150 ml
3	pink grapefruits, peeled and sectioned, membranes removed	3
2 tbl	white crème de menthe	2 tbl
as needed	mint leaves, for garnish	as needed

1. Combine all ingredients (except mint leaves) and ¼ cup (60 ml) water in a blender or food processor.

2. Transfer to an ice cream machine and freeze according to manufacturer's instructions. Serve in chilled dessert dishes, garnished with mint leaves.

Makes about 2 cups (500 ml), 4 servings.
Each serving: cal 217, fat .2 g, cal from fat 1%, chol 0 mg

Great Grapefruit

The tangy flavor of grapefruit sorbet makes a wonderful palate cleanser to refresh the taste buds between courses. The most popular grapefruit variety today is the seedless Marsh, which has a yellow rind and yellow fruit. Thompson and Ruby, the sweeter, pink-fleshed varieties, have gained popularity in recent years and make especially tasty sorbets.

Availability *Fresh grapefruit can be found all year, but quality is best and prices are lowest in winter.*

Selection *Pick grapefruit that feels heavy for its size. Avoid soft, puffy fruit with pointed ends.*

Storage *Keep grapefruit at cool room temperature for up to five days or refrigerate for up to several weeks.*

Strawberry Daiquiri Ice

The beautiful color of Strawberry Daiquiri Ice is as pleasing as its fresh fruit flavor. This still-frozen ice is quick to make because you start with frozen fruit, then let the food processor and your freezer do the rest of the work. The rum lowers the freezing point of the ice, which helps maintain a smooth texture. Garnish this speedy dessert with a swizzle stick or a sprig of mint. The recipe can be prepared up to 2 days ahead and stored in the freezer.

3 cups	sliced fresh strawberries or 1 package (12 oz/350 g) unsweetened frozen strawberries (do not thaw)	700 ml
3 tbl	light rum	3 tbl
3 tbl	sugar	3 tbl
1 tbl	lime juice	1 tbl

1. If using fresh strawberries, spread in a single layer on a baking sheet and freeze, uncovered, until frozen solid.

2. Place frozen berries and remaining ingredients in a blender or food processor. Process until smooth. If your machine struggles to process the fruit, let fruit stand 10–15 minutes at room temperature to thaw slightly.

3. Serve immediately in chilled daiquiri glasses or store in freezer until 5–15 minutes before serving, then place in refrigerator or on counter to soften slightly.

Serves 4.
Each serving: cal 95, fat .4 g, cal from fat 5%, chol 0 mg

GRANITA ESPRESSO

Use French-roast coffee beans for the best results. Stirring the granita as it freezes keeps it from freezing too quickly, producing even-textured granules. The texture of the granita should be grainy, not smooth like sorbet.

¾ cup	sugar	175 ml
1	cinnamon stick	1
3 strips	lemon zest	3 strips
3	whole cloves	3
3 cups	espresso or double-strength coffee, chilled	700 ml

1. In a saucepan combine 1 cup (250 ml) water, sugar, cinnamon stick, lemon zest, and cloves. Bring to a boil, stirring constantly until sugar dissolves. Reduce heat and simmer slowly without stirring for 4 minutes.

2. Remove from heat; discard cinnamon stick, lemon zest, and cloves. Cool to room temperature. Stir in coffee. Pour into a shallow metal pan and place in freezer.

3. Freeze until firm (1½–2 hours), stirring well every 30 minutes. Allow to warm slightly and stir one final time before serving.

Makes about 4 cups (900 ml), 4 servings.
Each serving: cal 164, fat .7 g, cal from fat 4%, chol 0 mg

WATERMELON SHERBET

Any of your favorite melons can be substituted for watermelon in this recipe. Be sure to reserve any juice that is released when you cut the melon into chunks.

¼ cup	sugar	60 ml
¼ tsp	salt	¼ tsp
1 quart	chilled watermelon chunks, seeds removed (about one 4-lb/1.8-kg melon)	900 ml
2	egg whites	2

1. Sprinkle sugar and salt over melon chunks and mix well. Once sugar has dissolved, taste melon for sweetness; add more sugar, if desired.

2. Purée melon, any juice it has released, and egg whites in a blender or food processor. Chill well. Transfer to an ice cream machine and freeze according to manufacturer's instructions.

Makes about 4 cups (900 ml), 4 servings.
Each serving: cal 113, fat .5 g, cal from fat 3%, chol 0 mg

SELECTING WATERMELONS

When purchasing precut watermelon sections for use in a summertime sorbet, look for firm, juicy red flesh and dark brown or black seeds. Soft white seeds indicate immaturity. Avoid sections that are cracked or streaked with white. With uncut melons, look for a smooth and slightly dull rind (neither shiny nor very dull), rounded ends, and a creamy underside. Miniature varieties are a good choice if you need only a small amount of melon.

ORANGE SHERBET

For an unusual and attractive presentation, pipe the sherbet through a pastry bag into chilled glass dishes or champagne glasses and refreeze until serving time. For a creamier texture, you can substitute skim milk for up to half of the juice.

2 tsp	orange zest	2 tsp
1 cup	boiling water	250 ml
4 cups	freshly squeezed orange juice	900 ml
2¾ cups	sugar	650 ml
3 tbl	lemon juice	3 tbl

1. Place zest in a fine strainer and pour boiling water over it. Drain, reserving zest.

2. In a saucepan over high heat, bring orange juice, sugar, 2 cups (500 ml) water, and lemon juice to a boil, stirring occasionally. Boil for 5 minutes. Remove from heat and let cool. Add orange zest.

3. Transfer to an ice cream machine and freeze according to manufacturer's instructions.

Makes about 4 cups (900 ml), 4 servings.
Each serving: cal 647, fat .5 g, cal from fat 1%, chol 0 mg

APRICOT FRAPPE

Translated from the French, "frappé" (rhymes with gourmet) literally means "chilled" or "iced". In most areas of the U.S. a "frappe" (rhymes with wrap) is a slushy frozen mixture made without dairy products. A simple sugar syrup is mixed with fruits or flavoring and partially frozen, then processed in a blender or food processor to the desired consistency. In New England ice cream is added to a frappe, and in still other areas a frappe is fresh fruit mixed with fruit juice and milk. The following two recipes represent two definitions of this icy dessert beverage.

| 2 cups | apricots, peeled, pitted, and chopped | 500 ml |
| 1 cup | sugar | 250 ml |

1. In a small bowl lightly mash apricots.

2. In a saucepan stir together sugar and 1½ cups (350 ml) water. Cook over medium heat until sugar dissolves (3–5 minutes). Remove from heat. Add apricots and let cool.

3. Still-freeze until mixture is firm. Process in blender or food processor until slushy. Serve immediately.

Serves 4.
Each serving: cal 230, fat .3 g, cal from fat 1%, chol 0 mg

PEACH FRAPPE

This milk-based frappe can be prepared with a variety of fresh fruit and fruit juices.

3	peaches or 1 can (15 oz/430 g) peaches in juice	3
1 can (5 oz)	undiluted raspberry juice	1 can (150 ml)
1 cup	milk, skim	250 ml
1 cup	crushed ice	250 ml

1. Peel and pit peaches. Slice each peach into 6–8 pieces.

2. In a blender or food processor, combine peaches, raspberry juice, milk, and crushed ice. Hold lid securely and process for 3 minutes.

3. Freeze until mixture is firm. Process until slushy. Serve immediately.

Serves 4.
Each serving: cal 62, fat .2 g, cal from fat 2%, chol 1 mg

SWEETNESS AND LIGHT

Low in fat doesn't mean low on flavor and excitement when it comes to the array of icy sweets you'll find in this section. Indulge in a frozen soufflé of dark cherries suspended in meringue, or enjoy smooth ice milk speckled with refreshing bits of peppermint candy. These delightful frozen desserts are as low in fat as they are pleasing to the palate.

Mango Mousse in Coconut Tulips

Coconut-flavored shells encase this frozen mousse.

¼ cup	unsalted butter	60 ml
½ cup	sugar	125 ml
½ cup each	flour and coconut shreds	125 ml each
½ tsp	coconut extract	½ tsp
1 tsp	finely grated lemon zest	1 tsp
¼ tsp each	ground cinnamon and ground cloves	¼ tsp each
1	egg white, at room temperature	1
5	ripe mangoes, peeled, pitted, and chopped	5
7 tbl	dark rum	7 tbl
1 cup	sugar	250 ml
2	egg whites	2
2 cups	whipped topping	500 ml
1 tbl	lime juice	1 tbl

1. Preheat oven to 350°F (175°C). Line a baking sheet with lightly buttered parchment paper. Have ready 10 miniature tart pans or custard cups (about 1½ inches or 3.75 cm across the bottom diameter).

2. In a heavy saucepan over low heat melt butter. When foam subsides stir in sugar and cook 1 minute. Remove from heat, stir in flour, coconut shreds, 1 tablespoon water, and coconut extract. Stir until smooth. Stir in lemon zest, cinnamon, and cloves.

3. Beat egg white until soft peaks form (see page 43). Fold one fourth of beaten whites into batter to lighten it, then gently fold in remaining whites.

4. On prepared baking sheet form batter into ten 2½-inch-diameter (6.25-cm) circles (depending on size of sheet), at least 3 inches (7.5 cm) apart and 1 inch (2.5 cm) from sides of sheet. Use 1½–2 tablespoons batter for each circle.

Spread batter with a spatula if necessary. Bake until edges are deep golden brown (10–13 minutes).

5. Let cookies cool on baking sheet 30 seconds, then remove one at a time with a large metal spatula. Working quickly, drape each cookie over an overturned tart pan or custard cup. Mold cookie gently over tart pan to form a flared tulip shape. Allow each tulip to set 2 minutes, then transfer to a wire rack to cool. Repeat baking and shaping with remaining batter. Place finished tulips on a baking sheet in the freezer until ready to use.

6. Place chopped mangoes in a blender or food processor and purée. Remove ½ cup (125 ml) of the purée; set aside. Add 5 tablespoons of the rum to remaining purée and mix well.

7. In a heavy saucepan, mix ¾ cup (175 ml) of the sugar with ½ cup (125 ml) water and bring to a boil over moderate heat. Simmer to soft-ball stage (see page 16). Meanwhile, beat egg whites until soft peaks form (see page 43). While beating constantly add hot sugar syrup in a thin, steady stream. Continue to beat until glossy and stiff (about 5 minutes).

8. Fold rum-flavored mango purée into meringue and then fold in whipped topping. Spoon mixture into a freezer container and freeze until firm (at least 4 hours).

9. To make topping for mousse, in a saucepan combine reserved purée, remaining sugar, remaining rum, and lime juice. Cook over low heat until sugar is dissolved. Remove from heat, let cool, and refrigerate.

10. To serve, scoop mango mousse into coconut tulips; drizzle topping over mousse.

Serves 10.
Each serving: cal 331, fat 9 g, cal from fat 25%, chol 15 mg

BEATING EGG WHITES

Some recipes in this book, such as Frozen Pumpkin Mousse (see page 44), call for egg whites to be beaten until foamy. Other recipes, such as Mango Mousse in Coconut Tulips (see page 41), call for egg whites beaten until soft peaks form. Still others, such as Frozen Lemon Soufflé (see page 45), call for egg whites beaten until stiff but not dry.

Soft peaks   The foam in soft peaks is thicker, whiter, and finer. When beater is lifted from bowl, whites form droopy, moist-looking but definite peaks. Use at this stage for soufflés.

Foamy   Egg whites are just slightly beaten; white suds begin to form in a matter of seconds. The mass is still transparent and liquid. Salt and cream of tartar (if used) are added at this stage once some foam develops. If these ingredients are added right away, the whites will need to be beaten longer before they will start to foam.

Stiff, but not dry   Some sugar is added now. With continued beating, foam thickens and develops a glossy sheen; it should still look moist. Volume has increased. When beater is lifted from bowl, peaks stand in stiff points. When bowl is tipped, mass does not slide.

Frozen Pumpkin Mousse

Canned pumpkin purée works just as well as fresh in this dessert.

¾ cup	sugar	175 ml
3	egg whites, at room temperature	3
pinch	salt	pinch
pinch	cream of tartar	pinch
½ cup	pumpkin purée	125 ml
¼ tsp each	ground cinnamon, ground ginger, and ground nutmeg	¼ tsp each
2 cups	whipped topping	500 ml
2 tbl	bourbon	2 tbl

1. In a heavy saucepan cook ¾ cup (175 ml) water and sugar over low heat, stirring occasionally, until sugar dissolves. Increase heat and cook without stirring until syrup reaches soft-ball stage (see page 16).

2. Meanwhile, in a large mixing bowl, beat egg whites until foamy (see page 43). Add salt and cream of tartar and beat until soft peaks form. While beating constantly, add hot syrup in a thin, steady stream. Continue to beat until meringue is cool (about 10 minutes).

3. In a small bowl combine pumpkin, cinnamon, ginger, and nutmeg. Mix well. Place whipped topping in a separate bowl and fold bourbon into topping. Fold in pumpkin mixture. Fold into meringue. Freeze about 4 hours. (If freezing longer, let soften in refrigerator for 2 hours before serving.)

Makes about 4 cups (900 ml), 8 servings.
Each serving: cal 131, fat 3 g, cal from fat 18%, chol 2 mg

Frozen Lemon Soufflé

The tart flavor of Campari, an Italian apéritif, makes this still-frozen dessert unforgettable.

as needed	sugar	as needed
3	egg whites, at room temperature	3
pinch	salt	pinch
pinch	cream of tartar	pinch
¼ cup	Campari	60 ml
2 tsp	lemon zest, very finely chopped	2 tsp
2 cups	whipped topping, well chilled	500 ml
as needed	chopped almonds, for garnish (optional)	as needed

1. In a heavy saucepan over low heat, cook ¾ cup (175 ml) of sugar and ½ cup (125 ml) water, stirring occasionally, until sugar dissolves. Boil until syrup reaches soft-ball stage (see page 16).

2. In a mixing bowl beat egg whites with salt and cream of tartar until stiff but not dry (see page 43). Beat in 3 tablespoons sugar, 1 tablespoon at a time.

3. While beating constantly, slowly pour the boiling syrup into egg white mixture; continue to beat until cool. Beat in Campari and lemon zest.

4. Fold one third of the whipped topping into the Campari mixture to lighten it, then fold in the remaining whipped topping. Spoon into six 5- or 6-ounce (140- or 170-g) individual soufflé dishes or a 1-quart (900-ml) soufflé dish. Freeze 4–24 hours. Garnish with almonds, if used.

Serves 6.
Each serving: cal 176, fat 3 g, cal from fat 18%, chol 3 mg

FROZEN CHERRY SOUFFLÉ

Freeze cherries when they are plentiful, and this treat can be a year-round favorite.

2 lb	dark sweet cherries, stemmed and pitted	900 g
1¼ cups	sugar	300 ml
6	egg whites	6
2 cups	whipped topping	500 ml

1. In a heavy saucepan crush cherries with ¼ cup (60 ml) of the sugar. Heat, stirring constantly, over medium-low heat until cherries are soft and liquid thickens slightly. Cool and purée in a blender or food processor.

2. Prepare a 4-cup (900-ml) soufflé dish by cutting a piece of aluminum foil long enough to fit around dish and overlap by 2 inches (5 cm). Fold in half lengthwise and wrap around dish to form a collar extending about 2½ inches (6.25 cm) above rim of dish. Tie foil in place with string.

3. In a heavy saucepan over medium heat, cook remaining sugar and ½ cup (125 ml) water, stirring until sugar dissolves. Cook to soft-ball stage (see page 16). While sugar cooks beat egg whites until stiff but not dry (see page 43). To make meringue continue beating and pour syrup into whites in a thin, steady stream. Beat until meringue is very light and fluffy and feels cool to the touch.

4. Fold cherry purée into meringue, then fold in whipped topping. Pour mixture into prepared soufflé dish and freeze until firm. Do not thaw before serving.

Serves 8.
Each serving: cal 237, fat 3 g, cal from fat 11%, chol 2 mg

FRENCH VANILLA ICE MILK

True ice cream aficionados always return to the rich flavor of vanilla.

| 1 recipe | French Vanilla Ice Milk Base (see page 51) | 1 recipe |

1. Prepare French Vanilla Ice Milk Base. Strain into a clean bowl and cool thoroughly.

2. Transfer to an ice cream machine and freeze according to manufacturer's instructions.

Makes about 4 cups (900 ml), 4 servings.
Each serving: cal 273, fat 3 g, cal from fat 10%, chol 111 mg

STRAWBERRY ICE MILK

Use plump, ripe strawberries to make the most of this summertime favorite. Use more sugar if the berries are less sweet, less if they are very sweet.

1 recipe	French Vanilla Ice Milk Base	1 recipe
	(see page 51)	
2 pints	strawberries	900 ml
¼ cup	sugar	60 ml

1. Prepare French Vanilla Ice Milk Base. Strain into a clean bowl and cool thoroughly.

2. Wash and hull strawberries. In a large bowl mash berries; add sugar and let stand for 1 hour. Add strawberries to strained ice milk base.

3. Transfer to an ice cream machine and freeze according to manufacturer's instructions.

Makes about 4 cups (900 ml), 4 servings.
Each serving: cal 366, fat 4 g, cal from fat 9%, chol 111 mg

IT'S THE BERRIES

The sweet, intense flavor of fresh berries makes them a natural choice for flavoring ice milks, sorbets, ices, and other frozen desserts. Whether you're incorporating berries into the base of your favorite frozen dessert, puréeing them for a sauce, or using them whole as a topping or garnish, fresh berries have a unique allure. Aside from the more common varieties—strawberries, raspberries, blueberries, blackberries, boysenberries, and cranberries—there are several harder-to-find varieties that you may encounter at a farmers' market or roadside stand: red or white currants, gooseberries, lingonberries, or loganberries.

Peppermint-Stick Ice Milk

This is a favorite among kids of all ages, perhaps because it is the color of bubble gum.

½ cup	hard peppermint candies	60 ml
1 recipe	French Vanilla Ice Milk Base	1 recipe
	(see page 51)	
1 tsp	peppermint extract	1 tsp

1. Crush peppermint candies into small pieces by wrapping them in a paper towel and hitting them with a mallet.

2. Prepare French Vanilla Ice Milk Base. Strain into a clean bowl. Add crushed candies and peppermint extract, mixing well. The candies will partially melt, turning the ice milk peppermint pink.

3. Transfer to an ice cream machine and freeze according to manufacturer's instructions.

Makes about 4 cups (900 ml), 4 servings.
Each serving: cal 380, fat 3 g, cal from fat 7%, chol 111 mg

French Vanilla Ice Milk Base

This recipe is the foundation for most of the ice milks in this book. Vanilla beans will give a richer flavor than extract.

4¼ cups	milk, skim	960 ml
¾ cup	sugar	175 ml
2	vanilla beans or 2 tbl vanilla extract	2
2	egg yolks	2

1. In a heavy saucepan, heat milk, sugar, and vanilla bean. (If you are using vanilla extract, do not add it until step 4.) Stir occasionally until sugar is dissolved and the mixture is hot but not boiling.

2. Whisk egg yolks together in a bowl. Continue whisking and very slowly pour in approximately 1 cup (250 ml) of the milk mixture. When smooth, pour back into the pan.

3. Whisk constantly over low heat until the mixture thickens slightly and coats the back of a spoon (about 5 minutes). Take care that the mixture doesn't boil, or it will curdle. Draw your finger across the back of the coated spoon. If the line your finger makes remains, the custard is done.

4. Remove vanilla bean; or, if you're using vanilla extract, add it now.

Makes about 4 cups (900 ml).

Frozen Persimmon Cream

The rich colors of fall come through in this lovely dessert. The delicate flavor of persimmon becomes stronger after the dessert has "ripened" in the freezer. You can preserve ripe persimmons up to 6 months by freezing them whole. Let thaw 20 minutes at room temperature before cutting and scooping out pulp.

4	persimmons	4
3 tbl	sugar	3 tbl
3 tbl	lemon juice	3 tbl
1 tbl	orange-flavored liqueur	1 tbl
3 cups	whipped topping, chilled	700 ml

1. Cut persimmons in half and remove center membrane. Scoop out pulp with a spoon (you should have about 2 cups or 500 ml pulp).

2. In a medium bowl combine pulp, sugar, lemon juice, and liqueur; mix well. Fold whipped topping into pulp mixture. Pour into a freezerproof bowl and freeze until firm.

Makes about 5½ cups (1.2 l), 6 servings.
Each serving: cal 107, fat 3 g, cal from fat 29%, chol 3 mg

Apricot Ice Milk

This rich, creamy dessert should be served in demitasse-size portions. Note that the mixture needs to chill for a day before freezing.

8	egg yolks	8
1 tbl	sugar	1 tbl
2 tsp	grated lemon zest	2 tsp
2¼ cups	milk, skim	550 ml
¼ tsp	almond extract	¼ tsp
1½ tsp	ground cinnamon	1½ tsp
1¾ cups	minced dried apricots	425 ml
¼ cup	apricot brandy	60 ml
8 oz	thick apricot preserves	225 g
1 tbl	lemon juice	1 tbl

1. Combine egg yolks and sugar in top of double boiler. Set over, but not in, simmering water and whisk well. Add lemon zest and milk, then cook, whisking constantly, until mixture is slightly thickened and has reached 180°F (90°C). Remove from heat. Add almond extract and cinnamon.

2. Combine apricots, brandy, and ½ cup (125 ml) water in a saucepan. Bring to a boil over high heat and boil until no liquid remains and apricots are very soft. Add apricots to egg mixture.

3. Combine preserves and lemon juice in a saucepan. Cook, stirring, over moderately low heat until preserves melt. Remove from heat, cool slightly, and add to egg mixture. Cool to room temperature, then cover and refrigerate 24 hours. Transfer mixture to an ice cream machine and freeze according to manufacturer's instructions. Store ice milk in freezer for at least 1 hour before serving.

Serves 14.
Each serving: cal 141, fat 3 g, cal from fat 20%, chol 122 mg

Honey Ice Cream

For maximum flavor, use fragrant, top-quality clover honey.

½ cup	whipping cream, light	125 ml
5½ cups	milk, skim	1.2 l
½ cup	sugar	125 ml
½ cup	clover honey	125 ml
½ tsp	salt	½ tsp
1	vanilla bean, split lengthwise	1
4	egg yolks	4
1 tsp	vanilla extract	1 tsp

1. In a saucepan combine cream, milk, sugar, honey, and salt. Scrape vanilla seeds into saucepan then add whole vanilla bean. Cook over low heat, stirring, until honey melts (about 5 minutes).

2. In a medium bowl whisk egg yolks. Add warm cream mixture to egg yolks gradually, whisking constantly. Return mixture to a clean saucepan. Cook over moderate heat, stirring constantly, until mixture reaches 180°F/90°C (8–10 minutes). Mixture will thicken visibly and will coat the back of the spoon. Do not allow to boil. Immediately strain into a bowl set over ice. Stir in vanilla extract and return vanilla bean to mixture. Stir until cool, then cover and refrigerate 24 hours.

3. Transfer mixture to an ice cream machine and freeze according to manufacturer's instructions.

Makes about 8 cups (1.8 l), 8 servings.
Each serving: cal 246, fat 8 g, cal from fat 27%, chol 126 mg

Frozen Lemon Yogurt

Lemon zest gives this dessert intense flavor.

4 tbl	sugar	4 tbl
1 quart	lemon-flavored nonfat or low-fat yogurt	900 ml
4 tsp	grated lemon zest	4 tsp

In a mixing bowl whisk sugar into yogurt until completely dissolved (about 2 minutes). Stir in lemon zest. Transfer to an ice cream machine and freeze according to manufacturer's instructions.

Makes about 4 cups (900 ml), 4 servings.
Each serving: cal 242, fat 3 g, cal from fat 10%, chol 11 mg

Plum and Zinfandel Ice

Serve this deep purple cooler on warm evenings.

2 lb	fresh plums, pitted and chopped	900 lb
1½ cups	Zinfandel wine	350 ml
1 cup	sugar	250 ml
1	cinnamon stick	1

1. In a saucepan combine all ingredients with ½ cup (125 ml) water. Bring to a boil over medium heat. Reduce heat and simmer until plums are tender (about 20 minutes). Skim off any foam that has formed.

2. Cool slightly and discard cinnamon stick. Purée cooked plums with their liquid in a blender or food processor, then strain through a food mill. Transfer to an ice cream machine and freeze according to manufacturer's instructions.

Makes about 4 cups (900 ml), 4 servings.
Each serving: cal 386, fat 2 g, cal from fat 4%, chol 0 mg

Yogurt-on-a-Stick

Match the yogurt flavor to the fruit or choose contrasting flavors.

2 cups	nonfat or low-fat yogurt, any flavor	500 ml
1 cup	puréed fruit, any kind	250 ml
1 tbl	honey (optional)	1 tbl

Mix all ingredients together. Pour into molds and freeze until mixture is mushy. Insert stick and continue to freeze until pops are hard.

Yield will vary depending on size of mold.
Nutritional values will vary depending on the ingredients used.

Pudding-on-a-Stick

These pops can be made from any size package of pudding mix, instant or cooked. Keep the recipe low in fat by using low-fat or nonfat pudding mix.

1 pkg	pudding mix	1 pkg
as needed	milk, skim	as needed

1. Prepare pudding mix according to instructions on package.

2. Pour mixture into paper cups and freeze until firm but not hard (2–3 hours).

3. Insert a flat wooden ice cream stick into center of each pop and freeze overnight. To unmold, carefully tear off paper cups.

Yield will vary depending on size of mold.
Nutritional values will vary depending on the ingredients used.

FRUIT-ON-A-STICK

Frozen fruit is quickly transformed into a tasty snack on a stick. Try experimenting with different combinations of fruit such as banana and orange, kiwifruit and strawberry, or pineapple and mango.

2 cups	frozen fruit (with or without syrup)	500 ml
1 tbl	sugar	1 tbl

1. Thaw fruit slightly, then mix with 1 cup (250 ml) water and sugar. Pour into molds.

2. Freeze until mixture is mushy. Insert sticks and continue to freeze until pops are hard.

Yield will vary depending on size of mold.
Nutritional values will vary depending on the fruit used.

Fresh Fruit Sauces

Colorful and refreshing, low-fat dessert sauces are a welcome change from rich toppings and gooey syrups laden with butter or cream. Made with a variety of fresh seasonal or frozen fruits and a few other simple ingredients you probably already have on hand in your refrigerator or pantry, these sauces are ideal for impromptu entertaining or a quiet night at home. They take only minutes to make in a blender or food processor; they complement most any ice cream, sherbet, sorbet, or ice; and best of all, you can make them as sweet or tart, as thick or thin as you like.

Melon-Berry Sauce

2	chilled cantaloupes	2
1 cup	fresh strawberries, raspberries, or blueberries	250 ml
1 tsp	freshly squeezed lemon or lime juice	1 tsp
⅛ tsp	grated nutmeg or freshly grated ginger	⅛ tsp
as needed	light sour cream or yogurt, for garnish (optional)	as needed

1. Halve and seed melons. Scoop out flesh, discarding shells. Using a blender or food processor and working in batches, purée melon and strawberries until smooth.

2. Add lemon juice and nutmeg and stir briefly to blend. Pour into serving dish and garnish with sour cream, if desired. Serve at once or refrigerate, covered, for up to 4 hours before serving.

Makes about 3 cups (700 ml), 4 servings.
Each serving: cal 105, fat .9 g, cal from fat 7%, chol 0 mg

Just-a-Bowl-of-Cherries Sauce

3 cups	pitted sweet red cherries	700 ml
½ cup	fresh or bottled pomegranate juice	125 ml
to taste	honey or sugar (optional)	to taste
½ tsp	almond or vanilla extract	½ tsp
as needed	light sour cream or nonfat yogurt, for garnish (optional)	as needed

1. Using a blender and working in batches, purée cherries with pomegranate juice until smooth.

2. Sweeten mixture with honey or sugar to taste, if desired; add almond extract and blend briefly to mix well. Pour into serving dish and garnish with sour cream, if desired. Serve at once or refrigerate, covered, for up to 4 hours before serving.

Makes about 3 cups (700 ml), 4 servings.
Each serving: cal 96, fat 1 g, cal from fat 9%, chol 0 mg

Kiwi-Nectarine Sauce

2½ cups	peeled, chopped kiwifruit	600 ml
1	nectarine or peach, pitted and quartered	1
to taste	currant or mint jelly	to taste
as needed	light sour cream or nonfat yogurt (optional)	as needed

1. Using a blender and working in batches, purée kiwifruit with nectarine until smooth.

2. Stir in jelly to taste and blend briefly to mix well. Pour into serving dish and garnish with sour cream, if desired. Serve at once or refrigerate, covered, for up to 4 hours before serving.

Makes about 3 cups (700 ml), 4 servings.
Each serving: cal 94, fat .7 g, cal from fat 6%, chol 0 mg

Pear Sorbet

Freshly poached pears yield a smooth, creamy, flavorful sorbet.

2 tbl	lemon juice	2 tbl
2½ lb	fully ripe pears	1.2 k
3 cups	sugar	700 ml
½	lemon, sliced	½
1	vanilla bean, split in half lengthwise	1
1–2 tbl	lemon juice	1–2 tbl

1. Stir the 2 tablespoons lemon juice into a bowl of cold water. Peel and core pears; place in lemon water.

2. Combine 3½ cups (800 ml) water and 2½ cups (600 ml) of the sugar in a large saucepan. Stir over medium heat until sugar dissolves and syrup comes to a boil. Reduce heat and add lemon, vanilla bean, and pears. Cover and simmer 5 minutes. Turn pears over and simmer until tender (5–10 minutes, depending on ripeness of pears).

3. Drain pears, reserving poaching syrup. Let cool. Purée in food processor. Chill 1 cup (250 ml) of the poaching syrup, reserving any remaining syrup for another use.

4. Combine ⅓ cup (85 ml) water and the remaining sugar in a saucepan; stir over medium heat until syrup comes to a boil. Cool to room temperature; refrigerate until cold.

5. Combine the 1 cup (250 ml) reserved poaching syrup, the 1 tablespoon lemon juice, and pear purée. Then add half the cold sugar syrup. Taste and add more syrup if mixture is not sweet enough or more lemon juice if needed.

6. Freeze in ice cream machine according to manufacturer's instructions. Cover and store in freezer for up to 2 weeks.

Makes about 4 cups (900 ml), 4 servings.
Each serving: cal 754, fat 1 g, cal from fat 1%, chol 0 mg

Cool Concoctions

From frosty Strawberry Blondie (see page 68) to Flaming Bananas Foster (see page 86), this section offers a frozen work of art for every occasion. Serve luscious Peach Melba (see page 81) after the theater, or delightful Watermelon Bombe (see page 76) for a backyard barbecue. These classic creations and clever innovations are eye-catching, scrumptious, and—here's the best part—low in fat, cholesterol, and calories.

GELATA CASSATA

This is a still-frozen version of a classic Italian dessert, cassata (see photo on page 4).

3 tbl	dark rum or amaretto	3 tbl
1 tbl	orange-flavored liqueur	1 tbl
¾ cup	mixed candied fruit, chopped	175 ml
1 recipe	French Vanilla Ice Milk (see page 47), slightly softened	1 recipe
¼ cup	pistachio nuts, chopped	60 ml
¼ cup	coarsely chopped semisweet chocolate	60 ml
1½ cups	whipped topping	350 ml
as needed	candied cherries and cocoa powder, for garnish (optional)	as needed

1. Combine rum, liqueur, and candied fruit in a small bowl; set aside for at least half an hour.

2. Meanwhile, line a 2-quart (1.8-l) loaf pan or mold with plastic film, pressing it well into the corners.

3. Spoon softened ice milk into a large bowl; fold in rum-fruit mixture, nuts, and chocolate. Gently fold whipped topping into mixture.

4. Pour into plastic-lined pan. Tap the pan against a cutting board several times to fill the corners. Cover with plastic film and freeze overnight.

5. To serve, invert the pan on a chilled platter. Lift off the pan and remove the plastic film. Garnish cassata with candied cherries or a light dusting of cocoa (if used). Cut into slices and serve at once.

Serves 10.
Each serving: cal 206, fat 6 g, cal from fat 25%, chol 46 mg

STRAWBERRY BLONDIE

For a quicker version of this classic ice cream soda, substitute 12 ounces (350 ml) of ginger ale for the seltzer water and ginger syrup.

5 oz	fresh ginger, peeled and cut into quarter-sized slices	140 g
1 cup	sugar	250 ml
12 ounces	seltzer water	350 ml
½ cup	Strawberry Ice Milk (see page 48)	125 ml

1. To prepare ginger syrup, in a blender or food processor and working in batches, process ginger until pulpy.

2. In a saucepan boil ginger in 2 cups (500 ml) of water for about 5 minutes. Set aside and let steep at room temperature for at least 8 hours.

3. Strain through a fine sieve into a clean saucepan, pressing hard to extract all the liquid. Add sugar and boil over medium-high heat until mixture is slightly reduced (about 5 minutes). Refrigerate until needed.

4. To assemble Strawberry Blondie, combine seltzer water, ice milk, and syrup according to instructions on page 70.

Serves 1.
Each serving: cal 102, fat 3 g, cal from fat 24%, chol 9 mg

ICE CREAM SODA VARIATIONS

Here are some traditional combinations that are sure to please ice cream soda lovers (all variations use either vanilla ice cream or ice milk): Black and White (low-fat chocolate syrup and seltzer water), Brown Cow (root beer), Black Cow (cola), and 50-50 (orange soda).

Making the Perfect Ice Cream Soda

During the heyday of the soda fountain, the skill of soda jerks was often measured by the quality of their ice cream sodas. One sign of a great soda was that its scoop of ice cream hung on the edge of the glass, rather than sitting on the bottom. If the soda jerk's technique was finely honed, the ice cream lightly touched the soda water, melting at the point of contact and flavoring the drink.

2. Fill the glass with charged water to within 2 inches of the rim. Mix well.

3. Position a scoop of ice cream or ice milk on the edge of the glass, balanced so that its bottom touches the surface of the soda. If you wish, add a swirl of whipped topping. Serve with a long-handled spoon and a straw.

1. Choose a suitably large glass. Put in about 2 table-spoons flavored syrup. (Use more or less, to taste.)

SPRINGTIME PARFAIT

A parfait made with seasonal fruits makes an elegantly simple dessert.

1 recipe	**Fresh Fruit Sauce of choice** (see pages 61–62)	1 recipe
1 recipe	**French Vanilla Ice Milk** (see page 47) or **Frozen Lemon Yogurt** (see page 57)	1 recipe
as needed	fresh fruit (whole berries or other fruits, chopped or sliced)	as needed
as needed	whipped light cream or whipped topping, for garnish (optional)	as needed
as needed	mint leaves, for garnish (optional)	as needed

Spoon some sauce into a parfait glass. Add a scoop of ice milk and a layer of fresh fruit. Repeat layers until parfait glass is filled. Garnish with whipped cream and mint leaves, if used.

Makes 4–6 parfaits.
Nutritional values will vary depending upon the ingredients used.

Make-Your-Own Sundae Buffet

The distinctly American creation known as the "sundae" is said to have originated during the days when a number of states enforced strict "blue laws" prohibiting Sunday sales of soft drinks, ice cream sodas, and other fountain specialties made with charged water. A clever Massachusetts entrepreneur is said to have concocted the "sundae"—which contained no soda water and therefore could legally be sold on Sunday.

Ideal for family celebrations or casual entertaining, make-your-own sundaes can be as light and healthy as you want. For a sundae buffet, offer several different bases—homemade or store-bought ice milk, sherbet, frozen yogurt—whatever you prefer. For an adult party, serve Strawberry Daiquiri Ice (see page 32) or Swedish Sorbet (see page 23). Choose an array of toppings from the suggestions on page 74 and sauces from pages 61–62.

Authentic soda-fountain glassware adds to the fun, but any good-sized serving bowls will do. Set the containers of ice milk and other frozen items in large bowls filled with ice or, for informal gatherings, use small insulated picnic chests.

Here are some delectable combinations to spark your imagination:

Base	Topping
Vanilla Ice Milk	Rum-soaked raisins Marmalade thinned with brandy
Chocolate Ice Milk	Crushed peppermint candies Sliced strawberries or crushed raspberries
Mocha Ice Milk	Almond-flavored liqueur dusted with powdered instant espresso
Frozen Yogurt	Pineapple chunks or kiwifruit slices

Low-Fat Toppings
for Frozen Desserts

A well-chosen topping can transform a simple scoop of ice milk, frozen yogurt, or sorbet into a spectacular dessert. For entertaining, make the array of toppings you offer as attractive and accessible as possible to encourage guests to help themselves. You can serve many of the following toppings in small bowls, although cream pitchers, gravy boats, or even small bottles make syrups, liqueurs, and other liquid toppings easier to manage. Large salt-and-pepper shakers make convenient serving containers for cocoa powder, ground cinnamon, and powdered instant espresso.

Try some of the toppings suggested here, then experiment with some new ideas of your own:

- *Fresh or frozen berries and other fruit (served whole, sliced, or crushed)*

- *Chopped fresh or dried fruits marinated in brandy, rum, wine, or fruit juice*

- *Chopped candied ginger or other candied fruits*

- *Crushed peppermint candies*

- *Crushed peanut brittle*

- *Multicolored sugar sprinkles*

- *Low-fat granola or other dry cereals*

- *Crushed low-fat cookies*

- *Maple syrup, honey, or fruit syrups*

- *Marmalade or jam, thinned with brandy or fruit juice*

- *Liqueurs*

- *Whipped light cream or low-fat whipped topping*

- *Shaved white or dark chocolate*

- *Cocoa powder*

- *Freshly grated cinnamon*

- *Powdered instant espresso or coffee*

WATERMELON BOMBE

This molded dessert looks like a miniature watermelon. It's a treat for the eyes as well as the palate. The bombe must freeze in stages, so preparation must begin early the day it will be served, or even the day before.

1 recipe	French Vanilla Ice Milk (see page 47), slightly softened	1 recipe
¼ cup	miniature semisweet chocolate chips	60 ml
1 quart	purchased raspberry sherbet, slightly softened	900 ml
as needed	green food coloring	as needed

1. Chill a 2-quart (1.8-l) melon-shaped mold in the freezer for at least 1 hour.

2. Line inside of mold with a layer of Vanilla Ice Milk. Cover with plastic film, pressing against the ice milk to seal it tightly and fill any air pockets. Return mold to freezer for at least 4 hours.

3. Stir chocolate chips into raspberry sherbet to simulate watermelon seeds; remove plastic wrap from mold and fill cavity with sherbet. Top with plastic film and freeze until firm.

4. To unmold, dip mold quickly in lukewarm water and invert onto a chilled platter. Return to freezer to set.

5. Paint outside of molded ice milk with green food coloring. Cover well and return to freezer. Slice to serve.

Serves 10.
Each serving: cal 237, fat 4 g, cal from fat 15%, chol 50 mg

CHOCOLATE-PEAR BOMBE

This elegant bombe boasts two luscious ice-milk layers surrounding a creamy pear sorbet center.

Pear Ice Milk

⅓ cup	sugar	85 ml
2 tbl	lemon juice	2 tbl
1 tbl	pear-flavored liqueur	1 tbl
1 tsp	grated lemon zest	1 tsp
1 can (29 oz)	pear halves, packed in	1 can (850 ml)
	natural juice or water, drained, puréed and chilled	

1 pint	chocolate ice milk	500 ml
1½ quarts	vanilla ice milk	1.4 l
as needed	whipped light cream and chocolate shavings, for garnish (optional)	as needed

1. In a saucepan heat sugar with ⅓ cup (85 ml) water until sugar melts. Remove from heat and cool. Add lemon juice, liqueur, and lemon zest. Chill. Stir sugar syrup into chilled pear purée. Transfer to an ice cream machine and freeze according to manufacturer's instructions. Let ice milk "ripen" in freezer for several hours.

2. Chill a 1½-quart (1.4-l) bombe mold in the freezer for several hours or overnight. Press three quarters of the chocolate ice milk into the mold, evenly covering the sides and bottom. Cover with plastic film, pressing against the ice milk to seal it tightly and fill any air pockets. Freeze until firm.

3. Press the vanilla ice milk into an even layer over the chocolate ice milk. Cover and freeze until very firm.

4. Fill in the center of the bombe with the Pear Ice Milk. Freeze until very firm.

5. Cover the top surface with the remaining chocolate ice milk. Cover with plastic film and freeze overnight or until ice milk is very firm.

6. To unmold, dip mold quickly in lukewarm water and invert onto a chilled serving plate. Return to freezer to set. Before serving, decorate the bombe with whipped cream and chocolate shavings, if used.

Serves 10.
Each serving: cal 208, fat 5 g, cal from fat 20%, chol 15 mg

FROZEN YOGURT TRIFLE

This new variation on a classic British dessert is easy to assemble.

1 pkg (10 oz)	frozen raspberries in light syrup, partially thawed	1 pkg (285 g)
1 pkg (10 oz)	frozen strawberries in light syrup, partially thawed	1 pkg (285 g)
2 cups	low-fat plain yogurt	500 ml
⅓ cup	sugar	85 ml
2 tbl	kirsch	2 tbl
1	8-inch (20-cm) packaged angel food cake	1

1. In a blender or food processor, purée raspberries and strawberries in their syrup. Strain through a fine sieve to remove seeds. Return to processor and add yogurt, sugar, and kirsch. Mix until smooth.

2. Spoon yogurt mixture into a shallow baking pan and freeze until firm. Tear cake into bite-sized pieces. Make a layer of cake pieces in a large glass trifle dish or glass bowl. Turn out the frozen yogurt mixture and cut it into ⅓-inch (.8-cm) slices. Place a layer of frozen yogurt slices on top of the cake.

3. Continue layering cake and frozen yogurt; end with a layer of frozen yogurt slices on top.

Serves 12.
Each serving: cal 330, fat 11 g, cal from fat 29%, chol 95 mg

Peach Melba

The great French chef Escoffier created this dessert in honor of a popular opera singer, Nellie Melba.

2 cups	sugar	500 ml
4	peaches, peeled, halved, and pitted	4
1 tbl	vanilla extract	1 tbl
1 cup	fresh raspberries	250 ml
1 recipe	French Vanilla Ice Milk (see page 47)	1 recipe

1. In a medium saucepan combine 3 cups (700 ml) water and sugar; bring to a boil. Add peach halves. Lower the heat and simmer, covered, for 10–15 minutes. Remove from heat; let cool. Stir in vanilla, then chill.

2. In a saucepan heat raspberries to boiling, stirring constantly and mashing berries with a spoon. Let cool and then chill.

3. To serve, place prepared peach halves on chilled dessert plates. Top each half with a scoop of ice milk. Drizzle raspberry topping over each serving.

Serves 8.
Each serving: cal 358, fat 2 g, cal from fat 4%, chol 56 mg

Just Peachy

The thousands of named peach varieties grown today can be divided into just two types: clingstone (peaches with pits that cling to the flesh until you cut them out) and freestone (with pits that detach easily). Clingstones generally have a more intense flavor and firmer flesh that keeps its shape even when poached.

Chocolate Madeleine Sandwiches

These sophisticated frozen sandwiches are made with madeleines, delicate shell-shaped tea cookies. You will need madeleine pans to make the cookies.

as needed	unsalted butter, softened	as needed
2	eggs, separated	2
½ cup	sugar	125 ml
½ cup	unsweetened cocoa	125 ml
½ cup	flour, sifted	125 ml
1 tsp	baking powder	1 tsp
pinch	salt	pinch
1 tsp	vanilla extract	1 tsp
1 pint	ice milk, any flavor, softened	500 ml

1. Preheat oven to 425°F (220°C). Lightly butter 2 madeleine pans (for 24 cookies). In a medium bowl beat together egg yolks and sugar until well mixed. Whisk in cocoa. In another bowl combine flour, baking powder, and salt. Fold flour mixture into yolk mixture, then incorporate 2 tablespoons unsalted butter and vanilla.

2. Whisk egg whites until they form stiff peaks (see page 43). Fold into batter. Fill each cookie mold two thirds full. Bake until madeleines are firm to the touch (10–15 minutes). Remove from pan and let cool on racks.

3. Using an oval ice cream scoop, place 1 small scoop softened ice milk on flat side of a cooled madeleine. Place another madeleine, flat side down, on top. Press together gently. Repeat with remaining madeleines. Wrap individual sandwiches tightly in plastic film and freeze.

Makes 12 sandwiches, 12 servings.
Each serving: cal 118, fat 4 g, cal from fat 28%, chol 26 mg

Vacharin de Cocoa

The crunchy meringue is an unexpected delight.

as needed	butter and flour	as needed
1 cup	confectioners' sugar	250 ml
6 tbl	unsweetened cocoa	6 tbl
6	egg whites, at room temperature	6
¼ tsp	cream of tartar	¼ tsp
¾ cup	sugar	175 ml
1 quart	ice milk, any flavor, softened	900 ml
1½ cups	whipped topping	175 ml
1 recipe	Fresh Fruit Sauce of choice (see pages 61–62)	1 recipe

1. Preheat oven to 180°F (82°C). Draw a 9-inch-diameter (22.5-cm) circle on each of 2 sheets of parchment paper. Place each sheet of parchment on a baking sheet; lightly butter and flour area inside circles.

2. Sift confectioner's sugar with cocoa. Beat egg whites and cream of tartar until soft peaks form (see page 43). Add ¾ cup (175 ml) sugar, a tablespoon at a time, and beat until shiny. Fold in cocoa mixture. Using a spatula, cover area inside circles on parchment with meringue. Bake until meringues are firm (1–1½ hours). Remove meringues and attached paper from pans and set directly on oven rack. Continue baking for another hour. Release meringues from paper with a metal spatula. If the bottom of meringue is sticky, return it to the pan and bake until dry. Cool on a rack.

3. Trim meringue to fit inside a 9-inch (22.5- cm) springform pan. Set 1 meringue in pan. Spread with half of ice milk. Place second meringue on top. Spread with remaining ice milk. Wrap and freeze overnight. Remove cake from pan. Spread whipped topping over cake. Drizzle sauce over cake and serve.

Serves 12.
Each serving: cal 242, fat 4 g, cal from fat 13%, chol 7 mg

CHERRIES JUBILEE

This showstopper provides a colorful, dramatic ending to any meal.

2 tbl	sugar	2 tbl
2 tbl	kirsch	2 tbl
1 tbl	cornstarch	1 tbl
1 can (16 oz)	pitted sweet or sour red cherries and their juice	1 can (450 g)
1 recipe	French Vanilla Ice Milk (see page 47)	1 recipe
½ cup	brandy	125 ml

1. In a saucepan over moderate heat, warm sugar, kirsch, cornstarch, and cherries with their juice until hot but not boiling. Put in a bowl and bring to the table.

2. Divide ice milk among 6 dessert dishes. Warm a ladleful of brandy over a medium burner or candle. Light a match, ignite the brandy, and pour it over the cherry sauce. Stir until the flame dies down. Spoon over ice milk and serve at once.

Serves 6.
Each serving: cal 324, fat 2 g, cal from fat 7%, chol 74 mg

PLAYING WITH FIRE

Flambéing (igniting foods that have liquor added) adds drama and develops a rich flavor in many desserts. Here are some safety precautions to keep in mind to ensure a successful flambé:

- *Always use a long kitchen or fireplace match for igniting.*

- *Never pour liquor from a bottle into a pan that is near an open flame (the flame can follow the stream of alcohol into the bottle and cause it to explode).*

- *Set liquor bottle away from cooking area after use.*

Flaming Bananas Foster

You can substitute two large fresh peaches, pears, or papayas for the bananas. Flambéing produces a dramatic effect, but use caution when igniting the liqueurs (see page 85).

4	bananas	4
1 tbl	butter	1 tbl
¼ cup	honey	60 ml
2 cups	coffee ice milk	500 ml
3 tbl each	rum and banana liqueur	3 tbl each

1. Slice bananas lengthwise and then crosswise into chunks.

2. In a saucepan heat butter and honey until bubbly. Toss bananas gently in sauce to warm.

3. Divide ice milk among 4 parfait or wineglasses.

4. Add rum and liqueur to bananas; heat on high for 1 minute and ignite. Spoon sauce over ice milk.

Serves 4.
Each serving: cal 345, fat 6 g, cal from fat 17%, chol 17 mg

STRAWBERRY-BANANA TOFU PARFAITS

When the fresh, soft variety of tofu known as silken tofu is flavored and blended into a purée, it is hard to distinguish from sour cream or yogurt. In these nondairy parfaits, tofu absorbs the flavor of the banana and vanilla to create a delicately creamy dessert that is especially elegant when layered with fresh fruit. Almost any fresh fruit in season can be substituted for the strawberries or kiwifruit. Try blackberries, peaches, pears, and apricots for variety.

2 cups	soft tofu	500 ml
2 tbl	maple syrup	2 tbl
½	ripe banana	½
1 tsp	vanilla extract	1 tsp
3 cups	sliced strawberries or kiwifruit	700 ml

1. In a blender or food processor, purée tofu, maple syrup, banana, and vanilla until very smooth and creamy. Pour into a shallow pan and freeze overnight or for 8 hours.

2. Just before serving, cut frozen tofu mixture into small chunks and quickly blend to the consistency of ice cream. Spoon into dessert glasses, alternating layers with sliced strawberries. Serve immediately.

Serves 6.
Each serving: cal 99, fat 4 g, cal from fat 29%, chol 0 mg

MILE-HIGH STRAWBERRY PIE

Any variety of berry can be substituted for strawberries in this quick-to-make dessert.

1 pkg (10 oz)	frozen strawberries or raspberries in syrup, thawed	1 pkg (285 g)
½ cup	sugar	125 ml
1 tbl	lemon juice	1 tbl
2	egg whites	2
1½ cups	whipped topping	350 ml
1	prebaked 9-inch (22.5-cm) pie shell or graham cracker crust	1

1. In a large bowl combine berries, sugar, lemon juice, and egg whites. Beat until soft peaks form and mixture is very thick (about 15–20 minutes, see page 43).

2. Fold whipped topping into berry mixture. Gently pile filling high in pie crust and freeze until firm. About 30 minutes before serving, transfer pie from freezer to refrigerator to soften slightly.

Serves 10.
Each serving: cal 205, fat 8 g, cal from fat 32%, chol 1 mg

Frozen Roulade with Berry Sauce

Fresh berries intensify the flavor of this eye-catching dessert.

4 cups	fresh strawberries, raspberries, blueberries, or a combination	900 ml
1 cup	sugar	250 ml
as needed	confectioners' sugar	as needed
6	eggs, separated	6
½ tsp	vanilla extract	½ tsp
2	egg whites	2
¾ cup	flour	175 ml
1 quart	ice milk, any flavor	900 ml
as needed	fresh berries, for garnish	as needed

1. To prepare fresh berry sauce, hull berries if necessary. In a saucepan combine berries, sugar, and 1 cup (250 ml) water. Bring to a boil, stirring and washing down sides of pan with a pastry brush dipped in cold water. When sugar is dissolved, simmer mixture 10 minutes without stirring.

2. Cool to lukewarm and strain through a fine sieve into a jar, pressing hard to extract all the liquid. Chill thoroughly before using.

3. To prepare vanilla sponge cake, preheat oven to 350°F (175°C). Oil and flour a 9- by 13-inch (22.5- by 32.5-cm) jelly-roll pan, then line it with parchment paper.

4. Set aside 2 tablespoons of sugar. In a bowl beat remaining sugar with egg yolks until mixture doubles in bulk and becomes light and fluffy. Mix in vanilla.

5. In another bowl beat 8 egg whites until soft peaks form (see page 43). Add ⅔ cup (150 ml) sugar and continue beating until stiff. Fold yolk mixture carefully into whites, then quickly but gently fold in flour.

6. Spread batter in prepared pan. Bake until golden and cake springs back when touched (8–10 minutes). Meanwhile, sprinkle a tea towel with confectioners' sugar. When cake is done, immediately turn pan over towel and let cake fall out. Peel parchment off cake, then roll cake in towel, jelly-roll style, and let cool completely. Do not unroll cake until ready to use.

7. Let ice milk soften at room temperature until it is just soft enough to spread. Unroll cooled cake back onto towel it was rolled with; spread ice milk over cake. Re-roll cake, lifting towel to help with rolling and keep cake tightly rolled. Work gently to prevent tearing. Wrap completed roll in plastic film and freeze.

8. To serve, let roll stand at room temperature for 10 minutes. Garnish with berry sauce and fresh berries. Slice with a serrated knife.

Serves 10.
Each serving: cal 282, fat 6 g, cal from fat 18%, chol 135 mg

---

CREATING
FROZEN ROULADES

Any kind of ice cream or ice milk can be used in a frozen roulade. For the best visual result, use contrasting colors for the ice cream and cake. Serve with a sauce of either a complementary or contrasting flavor. The following suggested combinations will get you started.

Vanilla Sponge Cake with low-fat chocolate ice cream and raspberry sauce

Vanilla Sponge Cake with Peppermint-Stick Ice Milk (see page 50) and marshmallow sauce

Vanilla Sponge Cake with Strawberry Ice Milk (see page 48) and kiwifruit sauce

INDEX